THE ANCIENT WORLD

The Japanese

Pamela Odijk

M

The Japanese

The Japanese

Contents

The Japanese: timeline

Prehistoric.
Jomon culture inhabited Japan. They were a hunting and gathering culture. They used stone and bone tools, and made pottery which had distinctive designs. In about 300 B.C., the Jomon culture was disturbed by the Yayoi culture who probably came from mainland Asia. The Yayoi introduced rice cultivation, a primitive form of weaving and wheel-made pottery. The Yayoi people fused with the Jomon people. The Ainu people arrived in Japan from China, Korea and Manchuria during this period.

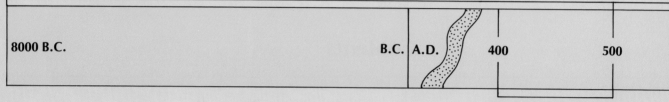

8000 B.C.   B.C. | A.D.   400   500

Yamato clan in Honshu becomes powerful.
Yamato ruler becomes emperor, and claims to be divine, tracing direct descent from the sun goddess.
Yamato family later establishes capital at Nara.

Kamakura period.
Yoritomo becomes Japan's first shogun. Mongols under Kublai Khan make two attempts to invade Japan.

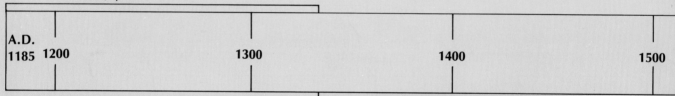

A.D. 1185 1200   1300   1400   1500

Muromachi (Ashikaga) period.
Kyoto becomes the great cultural centre. Zen influences felt especially in ink painting. Noh theatre develops. Civil war. Rise of commerce and manufacturing. Trade with China. Tea ceremonies become popular.

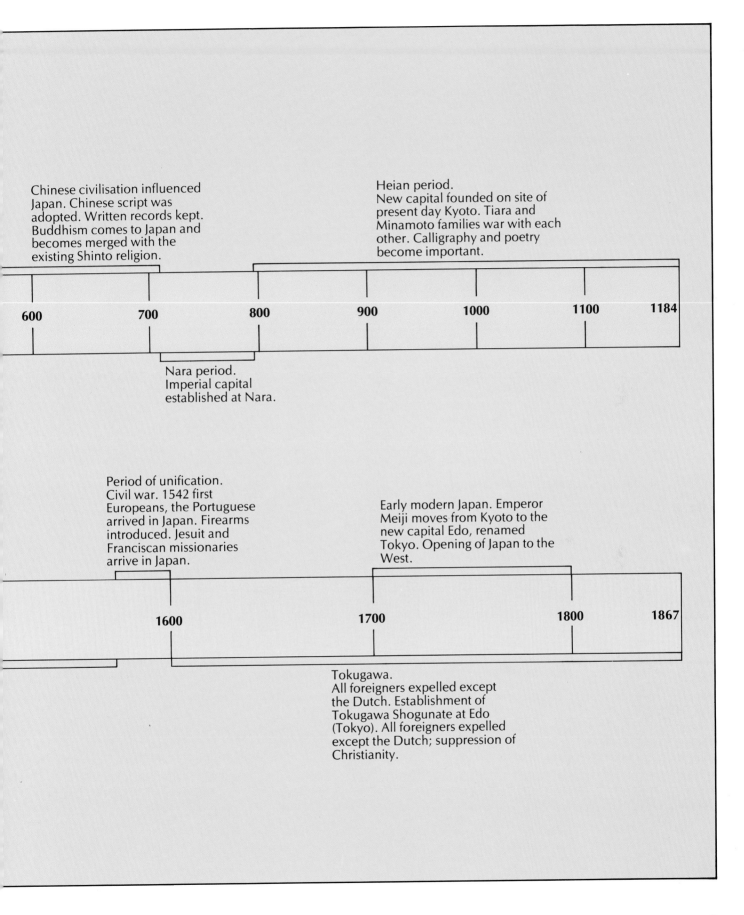

Chinese civilisation influenced
Japan. Chinese script was
adopted. Written records kept.
Buddhism comes to Japan and
becomes merged with the
existing Shinto religion.

Heian period.
New capital founded on site of
present day Kyoto. Tiara and
Minamoto families war with each
other. Calligraphy and poetry
become important.

| 600 | 700 | 800 | 900 | 1000 | 1100 | 1184 |

Nara period.
Imperial capital
established at Nara.

Period of unification.
Civil war. 1542 first
Europeans, the Portuguese
arrived in Japan. Firearms
introduced. Jesuit and
Franciscan missionaries
arrive in Japan.

Early modern Japan. Emperor
Meiji moves from Kyoto to the
new capital Edo, renamed
Tokyo. Opening of Japan to the
West.

| 1600 | 1700 | 1800 | 1867 |

Tokugawa.
All foreigners expelled except
the Dutch. Establishment of
Tokugawa Shogunate at Edo
(Tokyo). All foreigners expelled
except the Dutch; suppression of
Christianity.

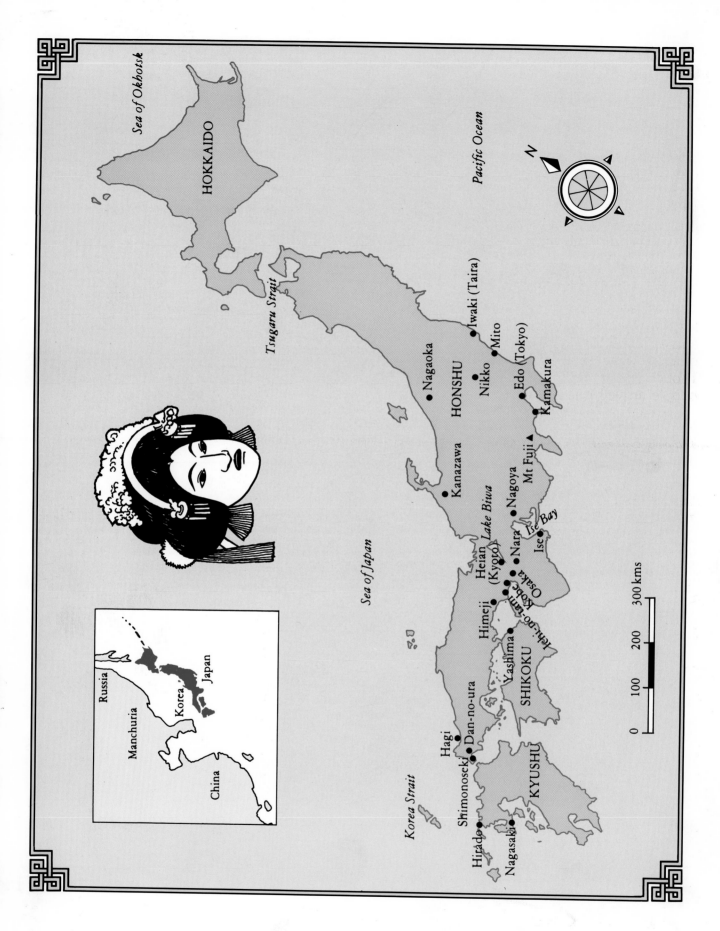

Sea of Okhotsk

HOKKAIDO

Pacific Ocean

N

Tsugaru Strait

Iwaki (Taira)
Mito
Nagaoka
HONSHU
Nikko
Edo (Tokyo)
Kamakura
Kanazawa
Mt Fuji
Nagoya
Heian Lake Biwa
(Kyoto) Nara
Ise Bay
Kobe
Osaka
Ise
Himeji
Ichi-no-tani
Yashima
SHIKOKU
Hagi
Dan-no-ura
Shimonoseki
KYUSHU
Hirado
Nagasaki

Sea of Japan

Korea Strait

Russia
Manchuria
Korea
Japan
China

0   100   200   300 kms

8

The Japanese: Introduction

Before the Chinese writing system was introduced into Japan in A.D. 461, the Japanese had no written historical records. What we know of Japan's history before this time comes from Japanese legends and folklore, and the work of **anthropologists** and **archaeologists**. From these sources, the early history of Japan is gradually being pieced together.

It is thought that the ancestors of the modern Japanese were Mongolian, and arrived in Japan from the Asian mainland by way of Korea about 2,000 years ago. They intermarried with other people especially the Polynesians. Though other people lived in Japan when these people arrived it is not known when the first people came to Japan. One group of early inhabitants that we do know about are the Ainu people, who arrived in Japan from China,

Japanese painting of a Franciscan monk. The Franciscan monks arrived in Japan during the period of Unification, A.D. 1573–1600.

Manchuria and Korea bringing with them a primitive culture. Slowly, the Ainu were pushed north, once the ancestors of the modern Japanese arrived. Today, descendants of the Ainu live on the island of Hokkaido.

The name "Japan" is thought to have come from the Malay word for island, "Japana" or "Japun". The Chinese named it *Jih-pen* meaning "the place the sun comes from". The Japanese use the term Nippon from *Nippon-Koku* (land of the origin of the sun), or Dai Nippon, Dai meaning great.

A **feudal system** developed early in Japan where the peasant farmers worked under a feudal landlord (daimyo). The peasant farmers, who tilled the land and grew the crops, were required to give the landlord a share of their produce.

Eventually a merchant class and a warrior class (whose members were **samurai**) developed. The Japanese were constantly involved in civil wars where powerful families, sup-

Japanese painting of Mt Fuji, the highest mountain in Japan.

ported by their samurai, vied for the right to govern all of Japan. Occasionally the Japanese would go to war against outsiders.

The two dominant religions in Japan are Shintoism and Buddhism. The Japanese followed the Shinto religion from very early times. Buddhism was introduced into Japan in A.D. 552, and became a very popular religion. The Japanese worshipped personal gods as well as nature gods, and often a rock or tree or a mountain would become a shrine. The Japanese also paid their respects to the spirits of their ancestors.

In A.D. 710 a site for a permanent city was selected on the Yamato Plain, and Japan's first capital, Nara, was established. The city was designed with wide streets where noble families built their houses, and Buddhist temples and monastries were built. In A.D. 794, Emperor Kammu moved the capital, first to Nagoaka and then to Heian (where Kyoto now stands). Heian remained the capital for almost a thousand years. During the Tokugawa period (1600–1867), a new capital, Edo (Tokyo), was established by the **shogun**.

Before the Tokugawa period Japan had some contact with the Western world as Dutch, Portuguese, Spanish and English merchants and missionaries visited Japanese shores. During the Tokugawa period the shogun closed Japan off to the outside world. No Japanese could leave the country and no outsiders were allowed in except for a small number of Chinese, Dutch and Korean merchants. The shogun feared the influence of foreign merchants and Christian missionaries. From 1850 onwards, though, there was increasing contact with Western people and this contact, over time, came to alter the way of life of the Japanese people.

Japan's history can be divided into the following periods:

10

Date	Name of period	Some important events
8000 B.C. to A.D. 500	Prehistoric	Jomon culture inhabited Japan. They were a hunting and gathering culture. They used stone and bone tools, and made pottery which had distinctive designs. In about 300 B.C., the Jomon culture was disturbed by the Yayoi culture who probably came from mainland Asia. The Yayoi introduced rice cultivation, a primitive form of weaving, and wheel-made pottery. The Yayoi people fused with the Jomon people. The Ainu people arrived in Japan from China, Korea and Manchuria during this period.
Classic Buddhist Japan 500–710 A.D.	Early Historic	The Chinese civilisation influenced Japan. The Japanese adopted the Chinese script and, for the first time, written records were kept. Buddhism was introduced to Japan and merged with the existing Shinto religion.
A.D. 710–794	Nara period	Nara, the first capital, was founded in A.D. 710. Strong Chinese cultural influence continued to be exerted.
A.D. 794–1185	Heian period	New capital founded on the site of present day Kyoto. Taira and Minamoto families were at war with each other.
A.D. 1185–1333	Kamakura period	Yoritomo becomes Japan's first shogun. Mongols under Kublai Khan make two attempts to invade Japan. The samurai or warrior class becomes important.
A.D. 1333–1573	Ashikaga period	Kyoto becomes the great cultural centre. Zen influences felt especially in ink painting. Noh theatre develops. Civil war. Rise of commerce and manufacturing. Trade with China.
Shogunate 1573–1600	Period of unification	Civil war. 1542 first Europeans, the Portuguese arrive in Japan. Firearms introduced. Jesuit and Franciscan missionaries arrive in Japan.
1600–1867	Tokugawa period	All foreigners expelled except the Dutch. Kabuki theatre develops. Arts flourish again. Noh theatre and tea ceremonies reach new stages of development.
Modern Japan 18th century	Early Modern Japan	Western learning through the Dutch. Education becomes available to everyone. Opening of Japanese ports to Western traders and visitors.

The Importance of Landforms and Climate

Japan is made up of a chain of 4,223 **volcanic islands**. The four largest islands — Hokkaido, Honshu, Shikoku and Kyushu — make up about 98 per cent of Japan's total land area. The Japanese archipelago is situated off the coast of the USSR, Korea and China, separated by the Sea of Japan. The Pacific Ocean is off the east coast of Japan. Most of the land is mountainous which makes agriculture difficult. Only 16 per cent of Japan's land is arable: this land is found in the short and narrow river valleys and on small plains. The Japanese have learnt to terrace the mountain slopes in order to increase the amount of land suitable for agriculture. Most of the rivers in Japan are short and fast flowing.

The highest mountain is Mt Fuji which rises up to 3,776 metres (12,388 feet). Japan's mountainous landscape has many volcanoes, some of which are active. The Japanese had to learn to live with volcanic eruptions and constant earth tremors. They adapted their lifestyle and architecture to withstand this constant threat.

Soils

The most fertile soils in Japan can be found on the coastal lowlands. The volcanic soils of the mountainous areas are thin and not suitable for crop cultivation.

Climate

Japan has a temperate climate with four seasons, though the climate varies from north to south. In the north the winters are long, cold and snowy, while the summers are short and cool. Moving south, the winters become shorter and milder, and the summers longer and warmer.

During the winter, cold dry winds blow from the Asian mainland to Japan, though north-east Japan receives monsoon rains which relieve the dry season. During the summer, moist warm winds blow from the Pacific, bringing plenty of rain. Japan is affected by summer monsoons that often cause much devastation.

Conifer forests on Hokkaido Island. In the background rise mountain peaks which are common throughout the Japanese landscape. Some mountains are live volcanoes.

Natural Plants, Animals and Birds

Because of the climatic conditions and the abundance of running water, Japan's plains and highlands are covered with thick vegetation. Evergreen forest trees, native camphor and cypress grow in the north while the warmer south has blossom trees and other ornamental trees. Wood from the forests together with bamboo are used for building, and to make practical utensils and ornaments.

In the high mountain areas, all vegetation gives way to stunted trees and treeless plains.

Except for bats, Japan's land mammals are of species distinct from those of the nearby Asian mainland. Bears, wild boars, badgers, foxes, deer, and monkeys, including the Japanese **macaque**, are native to Japan. In the high mountain areas live antelopes, hares and weasels.

Above: autumn colours of Kyoto, Honshu.

Left: Macaque adult with baby. The Macaque are native to Japan. Its thick furry coat enables it to survive in below zero temperatures.

Japan's native birds are mostly waterbirds. They include gulls, auks, grebes, albatrosses, shearwaters, herons, storks, ibis, ducks, geese, swans and cranes. Cormorants, some of which are trained to catch fish, have also found their home in Japan. Japan also has over one hundred and fifty species of songbirds. Other birds include hawks, falcons, pheasants, quail, owls, woodpeckers and ptarmigan.

The Sea of Japan supports a large variety of sea life, including whales, dolphins, salmon, sardines, sea bream, mackerel, tuna, trout, herring and cod. Crabs, shrimps, prawns and oysters are also found along the shores.

Japan also supports a variety of reptilian life, including snakes (most of which are harmless), turtles, tortoises, sea snakes, lizards, frogs and giant salamanders which can grow up to 1.5 metres (5 feet) long.

Crops, Herds and Hunting

Crops

The Japanese have been dominated by the need to make as much of their land as possible suitable for agriculture. The shortage of farmland meant that terraces were built on the mountain slopes, and land was reclaimed from ponds and marshes. Reclaimed land remained the property of those who reclaimed it for three generations. After that time, it became public land. In later times, the rights to agricultural land was divided between civilians and the military.

Rice was, and still is, the main crop grown by Japanese farmers. Because of the lack of good farming land, farmers grew rice in small paddocks.

Oxen were used to plough the lower flat plains, while the higher grounds were dug by men using primitive digging tools. To ensure good crops, both human and animal excrement were used as fertiliser. Rice was the main crop, while barley, millet and wheat were grown in areas unsuitable for rice paddys. Vegetables, mulberry trees and tea were also cultivated.

In the fields, the peasants wore a cape made of straw called a *minto*, which protected them from heat, cold and rain. The cape was made from overlapping layers of straw which came together at the neck. A cone-shaped straw hat was also worn as protection from the sun.

Rice Field Ritual

A ritual called *tasobi* was believed to ensure a good harvest. During the ritual, dances were performed, songs sung, the seed sown and special feasts organised to obtain the help of the *kami* (gods or spirits). A form of divination using an arrow helped to determine which farming methods were the best to use. The arrow was shot at a target and the angle of the arrow indicated which method should be adopted.

Herds and Hunting

Japan lacked wide expanses of grassland upon which to graze animals. There were few domestic animals: draft oxen and the occasional pack horse. The Japanese were not hunters as both the Shinto and Buddhist religions abhorred unnecessary killing and regarded blood as a pollutant.

The sea provided the Japanese with an abundant supply of fish and shellfish which added protein to their diet. Seaweed was also collected for food.

A Japanese Feudal Estate

The Japanese word *sho* meant land, usually rice land, owned by a nobleman or religious body. As an area under cultivation grew in size the number of tenants also increased. Most of these tenants belonged to the class of warrior-farmer and ranged from a small family living and working on the land to wealthier households who could afford to employ farm workers.

The feudal lord (daimyo) had a great deal of control over the personal lives of his workers or vassals, and often gave advice and direction concerning their marriages, friendships and pastimes. A warrior's first duty was to die for his lord but at the same time was not to expect any reward from the lord in gratitude for services.

The landlords claimed *rokubu*, "six parts in ten" of all land produce, while the tenant for his trouble and maintenance kept *sijbu* "four parts in ten."

Japanese feudal lord's villa in Yokohama.

How Families Lived

Family Life

The family was the basic unit of Japanese society, and everything centred around it. Success or failure of a family as a whole was dependant on the behaviour and efforts of the family members. Reverence for family ancestors was always shown.

The father was the most powerful person within the family. He had the power to dismiss members of the family from the household, to kill a child who was convicted of a crime, to sell his children into slavery or divorce his wife without good reason. Ordinary people only had one wife but wealthier men also kept **concubines**.

Women were expected to follow the "three obediences": to father, husband and son. Daughters could not inherit property. Women of noble birth were expected to live a life of seclusion except for arranged entertainments.

Detail from an early 17th century screen depicting Nijo Castle, home of the Tokugawa family in Kyoto.

Houses of the Nobility

The nobility lived in houses which were large and built on main avenues in towns and cities. Such houses were surrounded by white stone walls: one entered through a gate in the wall. Houses contained special quarters for the master of the house and for his principal wife. The house was built of wood and was rectangular in shape. Moveable screens divided the inside of the house into rooms. Outside walls were covered with shutters in summer, and bamboo screens in winter. Passageways and courtyards connected various sections of the house.

The families of feudal lords were required to live permanently in the capital. The lord was required to spend part of each year there.

The Japanese used little furniture: at most it consisted of low tables and cushions on the floor with a **brazier** for heating.

Floor mats called *tatami* were made from woven rice straw and were an important part of house design particularly during the 15th century. These mats were arranged in a creative and decorative way. The Japanese wore soft shoes indoors so as not to damage the delicately woven straw mats.

Apart from the moveable free standing screens, Japanese houses had sliding screens called *shoji* of translucent paper pasted onto wooden lattices. These screens were fitted into wooden slots.

Paper blinds covered the window areas which did not contain glass but transparent or opaque paper. Oiled paper was used in winter to keep out the cold. Paper lanterns were used as decoration.

Houses of Poorer Families

Poorer homes were similar in design to those of the wealthy but less spacious and without the elaborate gardens and courtyards. Ornaments and decorations might include an example of calligraphy or a blossom branch and a few paper lanterns. Fewer mats covered the floor and furnishings consisted of cushions and possibly a low table. Mats used for sleeping were rolled up and put to one side when not in use.

16th century artisan's screen depicting a swordsmith at work in his workshop.

Artisans

Those who did not work in the fields were engaged in manufacturing goods, which included textile typing, silk weaving, printing, armour making, sword making and lacquerwork.

Education

Education was limited to the male children of the nobility. However, education became available to all by 1872 when it was made compulsory. Despite this, all children did not attend school until the 1880s. At first children only attended school for sixteen months. This was later extended to four years, and then to six years.

Food and Medicine

Rice was the staple food and was eaten at every meal with fish, vegetables, seaweed, fruit and meat according to income and religion. Meat was rare and usually eaten only by the aristocracy and soldiers in early Japan. Fish was an important part of the Japanese diet and was eaten raw, boiled or salted. Soups containing vegetables, seafood and eggs were also popular. When available, the Japanese added wild fowl, duck, goose, pheasant and quail to their diet and pigs were also kept by some farmers.

Fine cooking was considered important and the food was served in many small dishes. Although portions of each dish were quite small, the total amount of food served during the meal was quite considerable. People sat on their heels or on mats at low tables. They ate their food from small bowls with chopsticks (called *hashi*) which were made from wood, bone or ivory. The wealthy had chopsticks made of gold and silver, as well. Meals usually began with a hot drink of rice wine called **sake**.

Powdered green tea was boiled and placed in a common bowl before an image of Buddha. This was later developed into an elaborate ceremony for Japanese society in which many rituals were carefully observed. Ceremonies took place in special tea houses and tea gardens.

Absolute cleanliness and good manners were of utmost importance. Even the order and quantity of bites of food were prescribed as well as the posture of the body at each stage during the meal. Ladies were forbidden to make a sound while eating or drinking while men were required to show their appreciation at the end of a meal by burping loudly.

Festive sweets called *higashi* were served from as early as Heian times. These sweets were made from sugar and rice flour and fashioned into delicate shapes of flowers and leaves. They were served on special occasions such as weddings and festivals.

Tea Ceremony (Cha-no-yu)

The Buddhist monks introduced tea to Japan from China and it was in the Zen monasteries that the ceremonial use of tea first became important.

Left: 18th century cup with image of Mt Fuji, used in a tea ceremony.

Opposite: informal tea house in the grounds of the Imperial Villa in Kyoto. The gardens were laid out in the early 17th century. The interior was designed to appear to merge into the garden. This building was known as Pine Lute Pavilion because of the sound of the wind in the trees.

The Tea Ceremony Rituals

Before entering the tea room, guests were required to scoop water with a bamboo dipper, and wash their hands and mouths.

The signal to enter the tea pavillion was given by the sound of wooden clappers.

When everyone was seated, the water for the tea was heated in a two handled urn made of iron. Extra charcoal was kept nearby in a wicker basket.

Green tea, called *cha*, was taken from a special lacquered caddy and placed in a small bowl.

The tea master scooped the hot water with a wooden dipper and poured it over the tea.

The mixture was then frothed with a bamboo whisk called a *chasen*.

The tea bowl was then passed to the first guest.

Each guest took exactly three sips, cleaned the rim of the bowl, and passed it to the next guest.

When the bowl was emptied it would be passed around again and examined as a work of art.

No trivial gossip was to be indulged in and no flattery was permitted.

No ceremony was to last beyond four hours.

Medicine

Early medical diagnoses involved observation, questioning and touching. Touch was the most important, and involved detecting heat, hardness and softness on the body. Treatments usually involved prayers, chants and incantations although medicines were used and given in the form of infusions and powders. Acupuncture and massage were also used to dispel pain. Monkeys were kept and used in experiments to discover the effects of various medicines upon them.

In A.D. 608, the first Japanese doctors were sent to China to study medicine. The Jesuits were the first Europeans to practice medicine in Japan during the 16th century, followed by the Dutch who taught Japanese medical students. It was not until 1857 that Japanese doctors who had been trained in Europe founded a medical school at Edo (Tokyo) which adopted German medical methods. Women found a place in Japanese medical practice from earliest times with Shinto and Buddhist nuns being permitted to attend the sick and female professors being appointed to teach medicine.

The oldest surviving Japanese medical text is a thirty volume work called *Ishinhō*, which deals with the treatment of diseases to various organs and parts of the body. It is based on an earlier Chinese work.

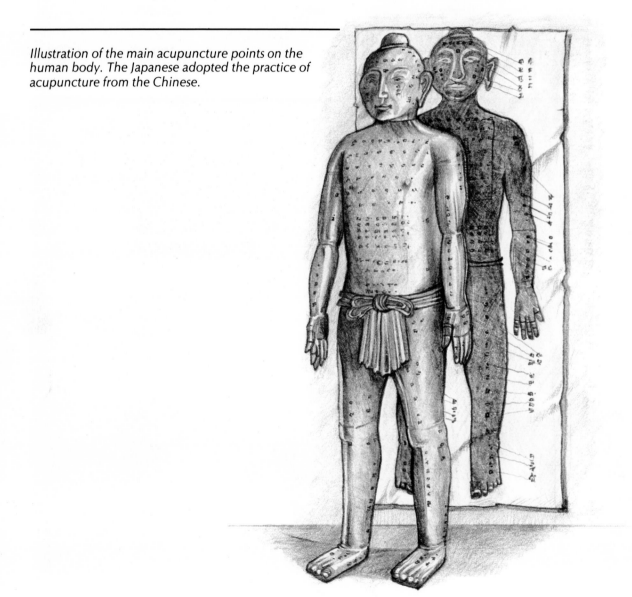

Illustration of the main acupuncture points on the human body. The Japanese adopted the practice of acupuncture from the Chinese.

Clothes

Japanese clothes were made from cotton and linen, and silk was worn by the wealthy. Earliest Japanese dress, from the 3rd to the 5th centuries, for men and women consisted of two-piece costumes with double-breasted jackets that flared out over the hips. These jackets were worn over men's trousers and women's pleated skirts. During the 7th and 8th centuries two piece costumes continued to be popular.

17th century pottery figure of a woman in traditional dress. Around the neckline can be seen the layered effect of wearing different coloured garments.

Imperial Dress

The emperor's court clothes were called *sokutai*. This was a formal robe. The emperor also wore an informal robe called *ikan*, and a robe for hunting and sporting occasions, called *kariginu*.

The emperor's formal robe (*sokutai*) consisted of inner trousers (*okuchi*), baggy white outer trousers called *uenohakama* which were made from damask, a *kosode* which was a long undergarment with short sleeves, a single robe, (*hitoe*), and *shitagasane*, a V-necked robe open at the sides. Over this was worn a loose outer robe called a *ho*. The *ho* was double-breasted, folded left over right, with large open sleeves, held in at the waist with a jewelled black leather belt.

The emperor wore a *kammuri*, a black cap made from lacquered silk as a headdress. Footware consisted of socks and slippers which were made from ox skin and decorated with brocade. The emperor's sword hung from a flat hand woven silk band called a *hirao*, and in his right hand he carried an ivory baton called a

19th century painting of a poet and courtier which shows the Uchikaka, a large outer kimono worn by women.

shaku. A fan completed his elaborate attire.

The empress's robe was called the *junihitoe*, an elaborate 12-fold dress. This robe consisted of an inner garment of white silk (*naii*), over which was worn a long red silk shirt (*uchibakami*). Then came a single unlined robe called a *hitoe*. Over this five long silk garments (*itsutsuginu*) were worn, one on top of the other. Then came the *uchiginu* of glossy red damask, over which was worn the *uwagi*, a long outer kimino of brocade that swirled around her feet like a huge fan as it covered the many kiminos worn underneath. Over the *uwagi*, a shorter kimono called *karaginu* made from figured brocade was worn. With this the empress wore a divided skirt called a *naga-bakama*, which covered her feet, and a long pleated train (*mo*) made from white silk and attached to the outer jacket. The many kimonos worn by the empress formed bands of coloured silk at the sleeve edges, neck and hem.

The empress wore an elaborate hairstyle (*suberakashi*) with special hair ornaments which included a gold lacquered chrysanthemum crest. A fan completed her official attire, too.

During the Nara period, the nobility imitated the dress of the Chinese and wore trousers and tunics covered by a robe. The basic kimino style was very like the robes worn by the Chinese women. The Japanese kimino was adapted from the Chinese.

During the Heian period the clothing of the upper classes was very elaborate and complicated with exact rules being laid down for proper dress. Men and women wore black trousers over which women wore many silk robes of different colours all carefully arranged in correct order. The rank of the wearer was shown by the colours. A wrong arrangement of colours was considered scandalous.

During the Tokugawa period dress became so elaborate that the shoguns frequently told the townspeople not to imitate the nobility by giving elaborate entertainments or dressing expensively. The townspeople compromised with this order, outwardly at least. They wore a plain outer garment which had expensive lining. This plain outer garment also hid the many expensive clothes worn underneath but which could be glimpsed as the person walked by. It was also common for people to change their clothes three times a day.

The Kimono

The kimono was given its special Japanese character by designers and dyers in the 17th and 18th centuries. The short sleeved kimono, called a *kosode*, was worn as an outer garment and belted with a small sash (*obi*). The kosode was fashionable from the 14th to 16th centuries. Samurai women also adopted a huge voluminous outer kimono (called a *uchikaka*).

Shoes

Out of doors the Japanese wore wooden clogs (*geta*) which were platforms on two wooden blocks. A cord passed through the clog so the

Ivory figure of a Japanese peasant woman. Peasants dressed simply, when compared to the wealthier townspeople.

wearer could place this between the first and second toes. These clogs came into common use when Buddhism, which prevented the killing of animals for leather, became a popular religion in Japan.

Slippers (*zori*) were woven from rice straw and consisted of a sole and a rope which passed through the first and second toes in a similar way to the clog. Zori were worn indoors.

Cosmetics

Cosmetics were very popular. In days of Kyoto's leadership men also rouged their cheeks, powdered their faces and wore perfume. Women used rouge and powder, and coloured their fingernails and lower lips. They also shaved their eyebrows and painted crescent moon shapes in their place. Folding fans, combs for the hair, parasols and swords were also a part of Japanese attire for the upper classes.

Religion and Rituals of the Japanese

Shinto

As with many early civilisations, the forces of nature — the typhoons, sun and earthquakes — were not understood and, as they could not be controlled, they were regarded as powerful gods who needed to be placated and worshipped. The first major religion to develop in Japan was Shintoism, which was based on nature. Trees, rocks, mountains and streams were worshipped as well as gods. Shinto shrines were built in groves or on hill tops. Mount Fuji was often climbed by chanting pilgrims and miniatures of the mountain were worshipped.

The sacred beings of the Shinto religion were the *kami* who were powerful spiritual forces that visited the human world and influenced it. The *kami* could only be seen if an appropriate receiving object, called a *yorishiro* was available. Such objects needed to be a particular shape: wands, trees, flags and swords were thought to be appropriate. Some humans were also *yorishiro* and became mediums. Offerings of cloth, horses, rice cakes, fish and other items were made to the *kami*.

It was believed that people who did not visit shrines or make offerings, fell into a state called *tsumi* which brought death and destruction. A *tatari* or curse was also believed to be placed on people for wrongdoings.

16th century Shinto god carved from wood.

24

Buddhism

Buddhism reached Japan, by way of China, in the 6th century A.D. and became popular. Buddhists believed in **reincarnation** and the ability to achieve enlightenment through strict personal discipline and meditation. However, the Japanese accepted only those aspects of Buddhism that suited their culture.

The Buddhist priests who went to Japan from China and Korea brought their elaborate rituals including chants, gongs, drums and incense as well as their holy scriptures (called *sutras*) and built their characteristic **pagodas** complete with images of Buddha. Buddhist altars called *butsudans* were located in Japanese homes. At the altars, candles were lit and incense burned.

As Buddhism became established various sects developed. Amidists, or followers of Amida, the Lord of Boundless Light, taught that people could achieve salvation by faith alone instead of good works. They also allowed their priests to marry.

This large stone Great Buddha was built by the Amida Buddhists during the Kamakura period, in A.D. 1252.

Hokke or Lotus sect Buddhists preached about outward strength. It was founded by a monk named Nichiren and this sect put their entire faith in the *Lotus Sutra*. This religion developed into a violent one and some followers roamed the countryside burning the buildings of other sects.

Another group were the Zen Buddhists who taught that enlightenment could be achieved by intense mental and physical discipline and concentration. It was popular with the warriors during the Kamakura period, and became a powerful religion in the 13th and 14th centuries when artists and intellectuals became attached to its teachings.

Gradually the two religions of Shintoism and Buddhism became merged in Japanese society.

Divination was also practised and there was widespread belief in demons, goblins, omens and spirits.

Important Japanese Rituals and Festivals

Birth

When Japanese women were expecting babies, special prayers were offered at Buddhist temples. Pregnant women followed a special diet and wore a special girdle which was blessed and given to them at the temple. After the child was born the mother was isolated from most other people for thirty-three days after which she again followed a special diet. She was not allowed to make offerings before the household Shinto shrines and her head had to be veiled whenever she ventured outdoors. Also following the birth of the child, other women would perform a purification ceremony by sprinkling the mother and floor of the house with salt and building a new fire in the house-hold cooking stove.

The birth of a nobleman's son was acknowledged with a ceremony in which the father, dressed in his court robes, held the child in his arms while receiving congratulations from friends and relatives. The guests also brought gifts and rice which were placed on lacquered trays beside him.

Detail from a large mural at the Monjudoo Temple, Kyoto, which depicts the Buddhist view of heaven and hell.

Death

Shintoists accepted that the dead went to a gloomy place called *Yomi*, somewhere in the middle of the earth. Buddhists believed in **reincarnation**, that is, being reborn in another form which was decided by the person's **karma**.

Bon

This festival was held from 13 to 15 July each year, and honoured the spirits of deceased ancestors. It was believed that at this time the dead returned to their birthplaces. Memorial stones were cleaned, dances performed and paper lanterns and fires lit to welcome the dead and to farewell them when their visit was over.

Shichi-go-san

This children's festival dates from early times. Boys and girls of three years of age, and boys of five and girls of seven, were taken by their parents to the Shinto shrine to give thanks for having reached these ages. Boys of the samurai class were dressed in a *hakama* or pleated skirt and presented to the feudal lord, while the little girls were dressed in traditional dress with a stiff *obi* over their dress.

Obeying the Law

In Japan, the ruler was the emperor (who was given the title of Mikado or "exalted gate"). Originally, the emperor ruled over the whole country in the same way as the emperor of China. Later the emperor was forced to delegate this power to the Shogun, or military authority. (Minamoto Yoritomo was the first Shogun in A.D. 1185 and Keiki, the last Shogun in 1867.) Under the emperor were various classes of people each of whom had special privileges, but this changed over time. Originally there were eight classes but in feudal times this was reduced to four:

shi	small educated ruling class
nō	peasants, who were the bulk of the population
kō	artisans who produced goods
shō	merchants who moved things from place to place and made them available for purchase.

Beneath these four classes were slaves, who were criminals, captives of war, and children who had been seized and sold by kidnappers or sold into slavery by their parents. Below this again was a caste known as Eta and despised by the Buddhists as they were butchers, tanners and scavengers.

Later the samurai became the most important class. The samurai was the warrior class and the society was organised as:

samurai or warrior class	
agriculturalists ⎫ artisans ⎬ merchants ⎭	People of these three classes were required to show respect and deference to a samurai. Failure to do so could result in being killed by the offended warrior.

Feudal Law and Reform

In early times, until 1721, each Japanese family was responsible for the good behaviour of each member. Feudal lords controlled their estates is much the same way, and people were punished for serious crimes. **Ordeal** was used in trials, and torture such as binding with tight ropes was a common practice.

The more enlightened Shoguns reformed the prisons and judicial system and set down better legal procedures. The first unified code of feudal law came into being in 1721.

Portrait of Minamoto Yoritomo who became the first Shogun in A.D. 1185.

Writing it Down:Recording Things

In early times Chinese was the formal official written language of educated Japanese men. This official writing system, called kanji, was also used by the Buddhist monks. Women were excluded from learning Kanji. Eventually a new Japanese script called hiragana (or *onna-e*) was devised which was less cumbersome than kanji, and this script was used by women. It was the Japanese women who wrote most of the early Japanese literature in this script such as diaries, letters, novels and poetry. Men also learned to write in this script, though they continued to write their diaries in kanji.

Another system of syllabic writing developed in the 9th century called katakana. By the 10th century written Japanese had become a mixture of kanji and katakana. By the 15th century the hiragana symbols had become popular and literary works were written in this script, while scholarly were written in katakana.

Calligraphy was considered an art and a person's handwriting was supposed to reveal their education, social standing and character. Japanese calligraphers were trained by suspending the arm with a cord from the ceiling so the arm holding the writing brush remained a fixed distance from the surface of the paper.

This scroll is inscribed, in calligraphy, with a text on hunting. The illustration is of an archer's equipment.

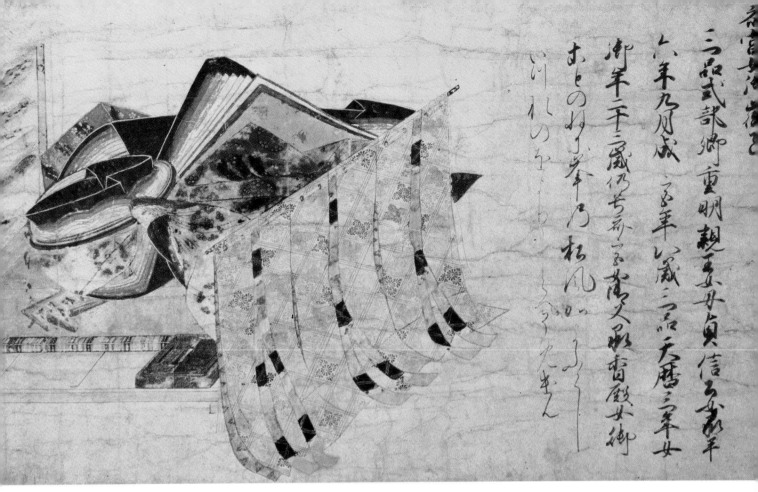

Portrait from a scroll painted during the Heian period of the poetess Saigo-no-Nyogo whose poem is inscribed on the scroll. The poem reads, "The breeze rustles the leaves on the hillside and seems to mingle with the tone of the koto. On which string of the koto, I wonder, does the breeze begin to play?". (The koto is a harp-like musical instrument.)

Newspapers

The earliest Japanese newspapers were the *yomiuri* of the 17th century which were sold by hawkers who read the newspaper aloud to attract customers. The first newspapers as we know them did not appear until 1861. It was an English language newspaper which later became the *Japan Herald*. The earliest newspapers printed in Japanese were the *Kanhan Batabia Shimbun*, published in 1862. This paper was derived from a Dutch newspaper in Java.

Papermaking

Japanese paper was made from the bark of the papertree. Young shoots of this tree were bundled and boiled with water and ash in a large kettle. When they had cooled, the bark was taken off. This bark was cleaned and boiled again in clear lyre and beaten to a pulp. Sheets of paper were dried from the pulp.

Recording Time

In about A.D. 604, Japan adopted the Chinese calendar system. Before the Chinese calendar was introduced, people calculated time by dividing the year into seasons which took into consideration heat and cold as well as the sprouting of new shoots and the falling of leaves. Each season was divided into three parts: increase in heat and cold, decrease in heat and cold, and the condition of the trees. Each of the three divisions was controlled by the cycle of the moon.

Japanese Legends and Literature

Japanese literature has a long history. The earliest surviving work dating from A.D. 712 is the *Kojiki* (*Record of Ancient Matters*). This work contained the first examples of classic Japanese poetry called tanka. A tanka was composed of five lines and had a set pattern of syllables: 5, 7, 5, 7 and 7 syllables per line, respectively.

Another important collection of Japanese poetry was the *Kokinshu* (*Poems Old and New*) completed in 905. This work contained many tanka poems, a form which had become very popular by this time. An example from the *Kokinshu* follows:

Honobono to	My thoughts are with a ship
Akashi no ura no	That slips island hid
Asagiri ni	Dimly, dimly
Shimagakureyuku	Through the morning mist
Fune wo shi zo omou	On Akashi bay

Longer Japanese poems are called *choka*. The greatest collection of Japanese poetry, the *Manyoshu* (*Collection of Ten Thousand Leaves*) was compiled during the 8th century. This work contained some 4,500 poems in several forms including the longer form, the choka.

The literature of Japan's Heian period (794–1185) was written almost entirely by women who used the hiragana script. Men, including the Buddhist monks, wrote in the rather cumbersome Chinese kanji.

During the Kamakura period of military rule (1185–1333), Japanese life was dominated by war. As a result the literature of the time was about fearless acts on the battlefield and other war tales. The authors of most of these remain unknown and it is thought that they were originally written to be chanted or sung by wandering minstrels. These popular tales were eventually written down by monks and scholars. *Heike Monogatari* (*The Tales of the Heike*) are examples of these. These stories also helped to establish the Japanese soldiers' fearlessness of death.

Haiku

During the Tokugawa period (1600–1867), poetry became even more refined, as the *haiku* form became popular. The haiku was composed of 17 syllables in 3 lines of 5, 7 and 5 syllables respectively. The essence of haiku was a blend of simplicity and subtlety. One of the greatest haiku poets who did much to develop the form was Matsuo Basho (1644–1694). Basho was a former samurai. Here are some examples of haiku poetry.

Yoshino nite	Come, my old hat —
Sakuro misho zo	Let us go and see
Hinoki-gasa	The flowers at Yoshina.
Harusame ya	A spring shower —
Monogatari yuku	While an umbrella and a straw raincoat
Mino to kasa	Pass by chatting.

The Novel

The Japanese novel began during the Heian period, with the publication of *Genji Monogatari* (*The Tale of Genji*) by Lady Murasaki Shikibu. This has become a great Japanese classic. This novel, written early in the 11th century, is about the life of a fictional prince. It is thought to have been the first great novel in the world and has been written about ever since. In the 13th century a commentary of 54 volumes on this work was published.

Early Legends of Creation

The earliest collections of myths, the *Kojiki* and *Nihon shoki* which are about the origin of the earth, the gods and the Japanese people, were written in Chinese.

The oldest Japanese legend tells how the god and goddess Izanagi and Izanami came down from the heavenly plains by a rainbow bridge and stirred the oily mass below with a rod. The first drop to fall from the rod became the first of the Japanese islands. The god and goddess stepped onto this island and created mountains, rivers, lakes and the rest of Japan. Their children were also gods and goddesses, three of whom were Amaterasu (Sun goddess), Susano (Storm god) and the Moon god. There are many legends and stories about these three gods.

The Wedded Rocks in Ise Bay are said to have sheltered Izanagi and Izanami. The straw rope which ties the rocks together wards off evil.

Japanese Fairytales

The first collection of Buddhist miracle stories, *Nihon Reiiki* (*Account of Miracles in Japan*) was written in the 9th century by a Chinese priest. These stories are also called Japanese fairytales.

One of the most famous Japanese fairytales is *Taketori Monogatari* (*The Bamboo Cutter's Tale*) which was written in the 10th century. This story tells of a childless man who finds a tiny girl in a bamboo stalk. She eventually grows up and becomes a beautiful woman and many men wish to marry her. As she does not wish to marry she sets them all impossible tasks with the promise to marry the one who can carry out his task. The emperor himself wishes to marry her but because he is the emperor she is unable to treat him in this manner. Instead, she dissolves into a ball of light and returns to her old home in the moon.

Art and Architecture

Because Japan is situated in an area subject to earthquakes and volcanic activity, buildings are designed to withstand destruction. In early times, the Japanese built very few high buildings. Although few buildings were rarely more than one storey high their structures covered a large area. Apart from houses, the Japanese built public buildings which had a distinctive style. The main types of buildings were palaces, castles and shrines.

Palaces

Palaces usually had several buildings connected by walkways and courtyards. They were built along simple architectural lines. Although none of the villas and palaces built by the Kyoto aristocrats have survived, an idea of the way they looked can be obtained from paintings and literature.

Castles

Japanese fortified castles were built during the 16th and 17th centuries by the feudal lords. The design for these fortress-palaces included barred windows, gates, trapdoors, and vantage points for firing guns and arrows. The White Heron Castle is an example of this kind of building.

Shintoist and Buddhist Architecture

Although Shinto shrines and Buddhist places of worship were often built next to each other, they were usually of contrasting architectural styles.

The Himeji Castle, also known as the White Heron Castle, was built in 1557 by Samurai Toyotemi Hideyoshi.

Sacred stone animals like this lion-guard-dog, were placed in front of Shinto shrines to protect them.

Shinto Shrines

In early times the Shinto religion had no buildings that were shrines. Instead, people worshipped at simple shrines which were rocks or trees, marked off by straw ropes hung with strips of paper.

In later times, Shinto shrines were simple wooden structures, raised off the ground on stilts, and consisting of a single empty room. These shrines were usually located in some quiet natural garden setting. These shrines were not elaborate as ornate figures were frowned upon. Also, no figures were used to represent gods.

Worshippers had to approach the Shinto shrines reverently, passing through a *torii*, which was a gate in front of the shrine that separated the sacred area from the public area. Sacred stone animals were placed in front of the shrine to protect it.

Buddhist Places of Worship

Buddhist temples were in direct contrast to the simple Shinto shrines. Buddhist places of worship were richly ornamented and carving was used as a decoration. The earliest Buddhist temples were built using Chinese architectural styles, as can be seen in the temple Horyaji near Narsa, which was one of the earliest temples built in A.D. 607.

Buddhist Influence on Art: Landscaped Gardens

Landscape gardening developed into an art form in Japan, largely through the influence of Zen Buddhism. The Zen priests designed the Japanese gardens to reflect, in miniature, the

33

Japanese landscaped garden with raked sand and pebbles.

world of nature. Everything in these gardens had a symbolic nature. The gardens contained *bonsai* which were dwarfed trees trained to grow in twisted shapes, volcanic rocks, mosses, ponds and lakes, and pathways which led to woods and retreats. The gardens were designed to induce a feeling of calm, peace and serenity as they were important places of meditation.

The gardens of Japanese teahouses were landscaped so as to create an atmosphere where people could gather with their friends in a secluded but pleasant retreat from the world.

Japanese Flower Arrangement — Ikebana

Ikebana (Japanese flower arranging) was a skilled art, and involved more than just an ability to arrange flowers. This art developed alongside the Japanese tea ceremony but became an independent art form in the 17th century. "Flower masters" taught men and women the correct way to grow flowers, how to admire their finer qualities and how to arrange them with thought to colour, grouping and line. The art of flower arranging developed from the early custom of offering flowers to

Buddha in the 7th century, and led to the establishment of the first school of floral art called *Ikenobo*. From the early styles, known as *tatebana* and *rikka*, develped all other styles of this art form. Later styles were called *shōka*, *seika* and *ikebana*. Today Ikebana is used generally to describe all Japanese floral art.

Originally flower arrangements were the domain of men, usually priests, warriors and the nobility. It was not until the 20th century that large numbers of women become involved in the art of flower arrangements.

Painting

Japanese painting was done on paper or silk, using ink or watercolours. Many paintings were preserved as *makimono* (scrolls), *kangemono* (hangings) or screens. Subjects covered in most paintings were usually nature, warfare or satirical paintings. Form and colour were the most important elements of Japanese painting.

Lacquerwork

Lacquerwork was introduced to Japan from China during the 6th century A.D. and eventually acquired a distinctive Japanese style. The earliest piece of lacquer known to have been made in Japan was the Tamamuchi Shrine. Lacquerwork was also inlaid with precious metals and shells. A process called *kamakura-bori*, which involved carved wood being thickly lacquered in red or black was popular during the Kamakura period.

Japanese landscape and flower designs were also produced in flat gold lacquer inlaid with pewter. Exquisite lacquered utensils used in the Japanese tea ceremony were made during the Ashikaga period (1333−1573). In the 17th century a school for lacquer artists was established at Edo and more processes and products were developed including the inro which was a small case attached to the owner's clothing. Eventually the inro became adopted as part of Japanese dress.

Other items which lent themselves to lacquerwork were cabinets, toilet cases, writing cases, stands, ceremonial objects as well as furniture and fittings in palaces and other buildings.

The lacquer used by the Japanese was processed from the milky juice of a special tree and was superior to that produced in China.

Metal Casting

Huge metal objects were cast by Japanese craftsmen. These included the enormous images of Buddha and enormous bells.

Netsuke

A direct contrast to this was the delicate carvings of netsuke. As well as being an indispensible part of Japanese dress they were fine works of miniature art. Originally carved from boxwood, netsuke came to be made from various kinds of material including ivory. They were worn as jewellery in the times when people below the rank of samurai were forbidden to wear personal ornaments.

Sword Making

Sword making became a highly skilled craft and an art. Not only were the sword blades sharp enough to sever a man's head at one blow but the handles were highly ornamented and inlaid with gems and precious stones. (The two swords which the samurai were permitted to wear were also a badge of honour).

18th century samurai sword made in imitation of a sword from the Heian period. The sword's scabbard is lacquered and has pearl shell inlay.

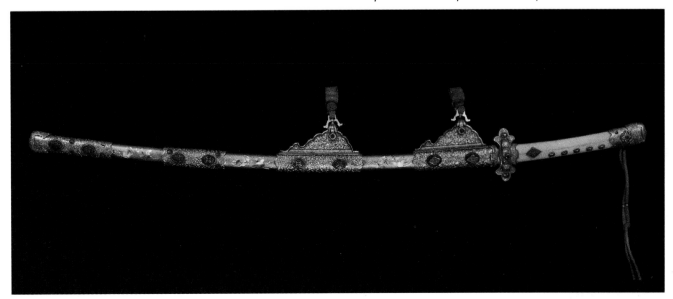

Going Places: Transportation, Exploration and Communication

The peasant people who were tied to the land and carried out their agricultural activities day after day rarely travelled. Trading by sea was not thought to be of great importance to these rice growing people as sea trade dealt with luxury goods rather than goods of necessity.

Trade

Under the military rule of the shoguns there were more opportunities for travel and trade, and, as such, more people became merchants and skilled artisans. Trade with China increased until the Mongols conquered China. Items traded included lacquerware, decorated fans, weapons, and sulphur from Japanese volcanoes. From China they obtained raw silk, porcelain, copper coins, books and paintings.

The Portuguese and Spanish traders and missionaries reached Japan by the 16th century but Japan closed its shores to all people during the 17th century. The Japanese banned all foreigners from coming to Japan except for a small number of Dutch merchants who were Protestant and considered by the Japanese to be less dangerous than the Catholics and their Christian missionaries. During this period of isolation, some Chinese and Korean merchants were also allowed into Japan.

Gradually Dutch scientific and technical books came to be read, translated and copied by the Japanese, and it was through these books that Japan became better informed about the West than other Asian people.

From 1854 Japanese trading ports gradually began to be opened to the Americans, English and Russians.

Roads

Because of the rugged mountainous landscape and the numerous islands, communication between communities was difficult but the Japanese were aware of the importance of roads. During the Tokugawa period (1600–1867), five highways were built. Some roads, like the coastal road from Kyoto to Edo had wayside tea houses, inns, and fine views of the countryside to make the journey pleasant.

The first railway from Tokyo to Yokohama was opened in 1872.

Ships

In very early times the people of Japan had only coastal dugouts and small ships. In 81 B.C. the emperor decreed that every province had to build a ship. Until the early 17th century Japan developed its ships but when the country decided to close itself off from the world, shipping and shipbuilding were halted.

1680 map of the Nagasaki port.

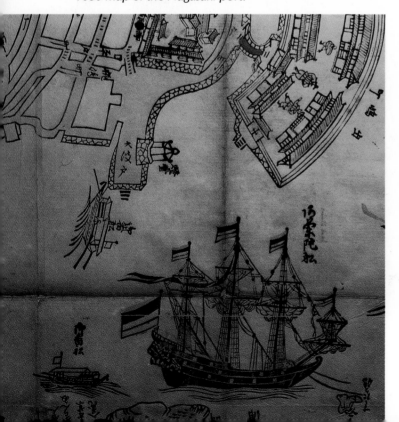

Music, Dancing and Recreation

Music

The Japanese developed their own unique musical instruments, many of which were introduced from China, Korea and India. Their instruments included stringed instruments, drums, mouth organs and flutes, and cymbals, bells and gongs. These instruments played together made up a Japanese orchestra. Japanese orchestral music was different to Western orchestral music where the aim is to achieve harmony. Rather, the Japanese sought to highlight particular instruments, and to reflect the changing moods of human nature and emotions. The musicians were highly disciplined in how they sat and held their instruments, and in how they played them.

Musicians performing Gagaku, ancient Japanese court music. Bugaku was the dance form associated with this music, and both became a part of Shinto rites.

Shinto Music

Special Shinto music (*mi-kagura*) was used in imperial palace shrines. Another type of Shinto music (*o-kagura*) was from large Shinto shrines, and yet another type (*sato-kagura*) was for local shrines. Shinto music had two purposes: to praise the spirits and seek their help, and to entertain the gods. Dancing was also a part of Shinto rituals.

Dancing

Dancing was very popular and greatly enjoyed in Japan, probably more so than in any other Asian country. There are accounts of whole villages celebrating occasions in universal dance. Professional dancers, both men and women, entertained audiences as well. Types of Japanese dances included:

Kagura	dedicated to gods and performed in villages, courts and Shinto shrines.
Gigaku	a Buddhist processional dance play using masks carved from wood which were painted and lacquered. Gigaku was brought to Japan from Korea in A.D. 612.
Bugaku	court dances performed by groups of four, six or eight male dancers. The dances had set movements and patterns. Musical accompaniment included drums, bells, flutes and panpipes.
Ennen	a secular form of Buddhist dance plays.

Kabuki

Kabuki was a colourful and melodramatic form of theatre which included music and dance and was more popular with the common people than Noh. Costumes were very elaborate and plays had themes in which common people were heroes and heroines. Kabuki actors would make costume changes in full view of the audience. Often the actors would wear stage costumes in layers with loose threads holding the outer garments at the shoulders. These would be pulled so the outer costume fell away revealing a more striking one underneath. Men played women's roles in theatre as women were banned from the Japanese stage in 1629.

One of the best known Kabuki plays is *Sukeroku* which is about a common person and a bullying samurai. Kabuki was popular because it offered an escape from the dull and monotonous lives which most common people were forced to lead at that time.

Bunraku

Puppetry also came to be very popular with the common people. This form of theatre came to Japan via Korea. Puppet plays were a combination of storytelling and shamisen music.

Noh

Noh was a distinctive type of Japanese drama which developed from dancing and singing performances in Heian times. Noh was presented on a simple stage without scenery. The theme of the play was usually an historical romance in which drums, flutes, elaborate costumes and poetry were used. Intricate sculptured masks were used by the actors to portray human and supernatural characters. Gesture, song and dance were used extensively in Noh plays.

Head of Banraku puppet representing a girl, from the Tokugawa period.

Other Recreations

The nobility who had more leisure time than the peasants enjoyed other recreations such as nature viewing, cuckoo watching, moon viewing and cherry blossom viewing. These group activities were often accompanied by sake sipping and poetry recitals. Good roads made journeying into the countryside easy and pleasant. Games such as shuttlecock, *utagarunta* which was a card game that involved matching the lines of 100 poems, chess and draughts were also popular. During festivals people watched fireworks, wrestling and side shows.

38

Wars and Battles

From the 11th century, during the Kamakura, period, the central government of Japan gradually became weaker and those who held powerful positions attempted to retain them with the help of powerful clan armies. The conflicts gradually became widespread and warriors became important in Japanese society. The samurai whose name means "one who serves" could be likened to an armed gentleman warrior who was highly trained in the art of war. Samurai became a dominant force in Japanese life. Originally a samurai was a warrior serving a feudal lord (*daimyo*). The samurai were bound by a code of supreme loyalty known as *bushido* or "the way of the warrior", to their superiors especially the powerful Minamoto and Taira families. The samurai warrior would rather die than be defeated or captured which was regarded as the ultimate disgrace. From this the tradition of suicide using a sword (called *hara-kiri* or *seppuku*), was preferrable to being captured. The code of the samurai was to serve the master and ask for nothing in return.

In spite of the training and respect given to all samurai, they received very little education and few could read and write.

Dress of the Samurai

The samurai had a strict code of dress. When not fighting, they dressed in two kiminos and a pleated skirt. Around their waist they wore a belt which had two swords attached to it. On their feet they wore sandals. Their hair was worn swept back with a headband, or plaited with ribbons.

In battle, samurai wore an armour made from small iron scales which were laced together. The armour consisted of shin guards made of cloth or leather and reinforced with steel strips, and thigh guards for mounted samurai; an upper armour of rows of iron lamellae which also had skirt panels; metal protective sleeves of chain mail attached to heavy cloth by braided silk cord; metal shoulder guards; an iron collar; a lacquered iron face mask depicting a fierce face to intimidate the enemy; and a cotton skull cap over which a helmet made from riveted metal was worn.

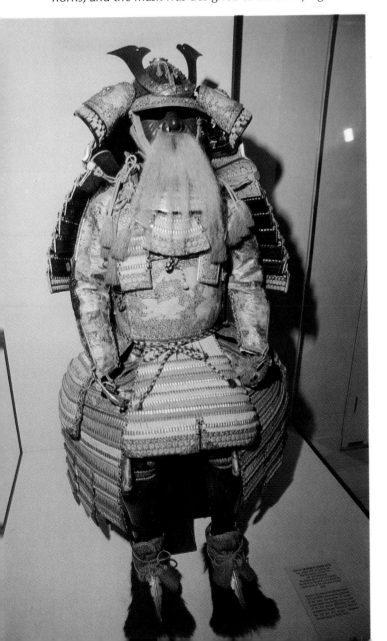

12th century armour of a samurai. The helmet has horns, and the mask was designed to be terrifying.

Detail from a 16th century artisan's screen depicting an armourer at work. The various pieces of the samurai's armour are fashioned by the craftsmen and apprentices.

The samurai armour was usually quite striking. The iron scales were lacquered using bright colours, and sewn together using a contrasting silk cord.

Battle headdress was a full protective mask which was moulded to represent the wearer's face contorted and menacing with rage. Some masks had horns, too.

Swords

The two-handed samurai sword was the supreme and revered weapon of war and was thought to have a life and spirit of its own. Samurai were highly skilled swordsmen and practised for hours each day with their weapon. They could severe a man's head with a single blow. Soldiers who were defeated in battle often prayed at the shrine of Hachiman, the war god, to ask why their sword had lost its spirit. Sword makers in Japan were regarded as an honoured class.

War Against the Mongols

In 1274 Genghis Khan's grandson, Kublai Khan, reached two small Japanese islands in a fleet built for his Mongol warriors by the Koreans. The local Japanese samurai fought them but were defeated by their superior battle tactics and by the superior weapons of the Mongols which included crossbows that could shoot bolts much further than the Japanese arrows and by their superior battle tactics.

Although there were several small battles against the Mongols, the main attack did not occur until 1281, when, after a fifty day intense battle involving large armies of Mongols and samurai, a typhoon (called the *kamikaze* or "divine wind") destroyed the enemy fleet, and marooned many of the Mongols, enabling the Japanese to be victorious.

Japanese Inventions and Special Skills

Japanese Writing

Because Chinese characters could not express the Japanese language satisfactorily, a Japanese script called *hiragana* was devised. This was used by women who had been previously excluded from learning the Chinese script *kanji* which was the original official written language of educated Japanese men. *Katakanga*, another system of syllabic writing, was also developed. Literary works began to be written in hiragana while practical and scholarly books were written in *katakana*. (Katakana was later used in notes that were typed or printed with machines.)

Lacquerwork

Although introduced from China, the Japanese developed a unique style and quality of lacquerwork superior to that of the Chinese. With the increase in popularity of the tea ceremony, lacquerwork artists and craftsmen competed to produce articles of high quality and artistic merit.

Tea Ceremony (Cha-no-yu)

Tea drinking which originated in China was introduced to Japan by the Buddhist monks. It became an active part of Buddhist rituals. By the 15th century the tea ceremony had moved away from being a strictly religious ritual as Japanese people gathered with their friends to drink tea and discuss the arts. Gradually the special tea ceremony rituals became a special part of Japanese culture. The special utensils became art objects in themselves, and ceremonies were conducted in special tea houses and tea rooms.

Landscape Gardening

Although derived from the Chinese, the Japanese garden developed a unique style. They were either hill gardens or flat gardens. The hill garden contained hills and ponds and became the ideal associated with Mt Fuji. The flat garden represented the lake or sea surrounded by islands. Landscape gardeners attempted to capture the spirit of the landscape which was reproduced in the garden and much attention was given to detail. Some gardens were scaled down to 30 square centimetres (12 square inches). Gardens were classified as elaborate, moderate and modest, and each had prescribed rules.

Stones were also used in Japanese gardens. Nine stones, five standing and four lying were used in Buddhist gardens to represent nine spirits. Such Japanese gardens eventually had an influence on Western gardens.

Miniaturisation

From clothing to the decorations on parasols, fans, *inro*, *netsuke* and wood carvings, the Japanese excelled in the art of delicate miniature decoration. Landscape gardens, some of which were scaled down to a minute size, show this same skill. It is also found in the delicate, painstaking and exacting art of *bonsai*, the Japanese mature dwarf tree. Although bonsai as an art originated in China, it was developed by the Japanese.

Why the Civilisation Declined

From the mid 16th century onwards, the Europeans intruded into Japanese lands and imposed themselves on the people and culture. The first Europeans to reach Japan were the Portuguese traders who were well received by the Japanese. The Portuguese Jesuit missionaries followed and although they were welcomed by the Japanese, they turned their attention to China instead and began their mission work there more earnestly. However, their accurate and detailed accounts of Japanese life have been very valuable to later scholars. Later though, the Jesuits returned to Japan and gained some converts to Christianity. The Spanish Franciscans also reached Japan with their particular methods of trying to win Christian converts. Many Japanese who were converted to Christianity were persecuted.

Soon Japanese authorities became suspicious of all intruders and expelled them (although many Jesuits went into hiding). Japan again became an isolated culture having little to do with the outside world for about two centuries.

In 1600 the Dutch ship *Liefde* landed at Beppu Bay in Kyushu with an English pilot named Will Adams. The Dutch had been given permission to establish a trading port at Hirado in Kyushu and the Dutch continued to visit there throughout Japan's two centuries of isolation.

From the 1850s onwards there was increasing contact with people of Western nations. By this time, too, the warships and weapons of the West were superior to those of the Japanese so it was not possible to keep the foreigners out by force.

Because of the Western contact, and contact with other Asian people, the Russians, and the eventual industrialisation of Japan which followed, the Japanese civilisation and the *Yamato Damashii*, or "Spirit of Old Japan", was changed for all time.

Detail from a 16th century Japanese screen showing Portuguese traders and Jesuit missionaries bathing.

Glossary

Archaeologists   People who study cultures, especially prehistoric cultures, by examining artefacts that are excavated, and dating them.

Anthropologists   People who study the science of human beginnings.

Artisan   Craftspeople who create or produce goods for merchants to sell in other districts, or to ship abroad.

Bodhisattva   An enlightened person who delays their entry to Nirvana, so as to come back to earth to help others attain enlightenment.

Brazier   A metal receptacle for holding burning charcoal or other fuel; used for heating rooms.

Bushido   The name given to the samurai code of honour. The name means "the Way of the Warrior".

Butsudan   A household Buddhist altar where incense was burned, candles lit and family ancestors remembered. During the 17th century, Buddhist priests would inspect these altars to see if they were being properly maintained.

Concubines   Secondary wives who lived in a man's house without being legally married to him.

Emperor   The Japanese emperor ruled over the whole country as head of the bureaucracy in the same manner as the emperor of China. At the same time he was the traditional high priest who made peace with the gods for the benefit of his people. The shoguns or military rulers replaced the emperor as ruler from 1185 to 1867 after which the emperor was restored to power.

Enlightenment   A Buddhist belief which meant the discovering of the inner meaning of life.

Feudal System   A system by which society was organised. In Japan the peasants belonged to the land on which they worked and the landlord (*daimyō*) who owned the land also owned the peasants. The peasants worked the land and paid a proportion of their crops to the feudal lord as rent.

Karma   A Buddhist belief that a person's status in life has been determined by his or her deeds in a previous life or incarnation, and that one's actions in this life determine one's status in the next life.

Meditation   A period of quiet reflection and contemplation practised by Buddhists in order to bring the person inner peace and understanding.

Ordeal   A form of trial where an accused person is subjected to a harsh test involving fire or water to see if they are innocent or guilty. The result was believed to be a divine judgement.

Pagoda   (or drum tower). These were a part of Buddhist temples. They were towers reaching up to twelve storeys, with each storey diminishing in size, with a mast at the top ringed with metal discs.

Pilgrims   Followers of a religion who journey to a sacred spot. Followers of both Shinto and Buddhism made pilgrimages.

Reincarnation   A Buddhist belief that the soul, upon death of the body, moves to another body or form.

Sake   A rice wine. Meals usually began with a hot drink of sake.

Samurai   One of the Japanese warrior caste who became particularly powerful during the 11th century. The name Samurai means "One who serves".

Serfs   Peasants who worked for a feudal lord. In early Japanese society, the peasants tilled the land. They were in the service of a feudal lord (called a daimyō) to whom they were required to pay part of his crop.

Shogun   The name given to the head of the ruling government as against the emperor who was only a figure head. Various shoguns ruled until 1867 when the emperor was returned to power.

The Japanese: Some Famous People and Places

Fijiwara Family

This was one of the most remarkable of all Japanese families who dominated the Imperial government during the Heian period, A.D. 791 to 1185. This dynasty was founded by Nakatomi Kamatari (614–669). For protecting the successor to the Imperial throne, the prince bestowed the family name of Fijiwara. The family developed four branches. The Fijiwara family cultivated special relationships with the Imperial family by marrying daughters to emperors, and also gained further influence through the Buddhist religion. They acquired and controlled large areas of land.

For three hundred years the Fijiwara dominated, opposing violence and regarded the uneducated Japanese warriors as inferior. However, they were eventually defeated by the military of the Shirakawa family in 1159.

Tokugawa Family

This family controlled the government under fifteen shoguns from 1603 until the Meiji restoration in 1868. The family was descended from a son of Emperor Seiwa of the 9th century. In 1600, at the battle of Sekigahara, Tokugawa Ieyasu defeated the troops of Toyotomi Hideyori. The first and third shoguns were buried at Nikko and the others at Tokyo.

A grandson of Tokugawa Ieyasu, Tokugawa Mitsukuni, became a local governor and spent almost one third of his area's income having a 240 volume history of Japan compiled by eminent scholars. He also excavated many tombs in the interests of research.

The Tokugawa or Edo period was a time of peace and prosperity, when arts and learning flourished. The Tokugawa shoguns moved the military government from Kyoto to Edo (modern Tokyo) and closed Japan to all foreigners except the Dutch and Chinese, and prohibited the practice of Christianity.

Heian

Heian, built on the island of Honshu, was the capital of Japan from A.D. 796 to 1869 and called the Capital of Tranquillity and Peace. The city was an addition to the great palace of Heian-jō, (the Castle of Tranquillity and Peace) and was named Heian-Kyō, and sometimes called Kyoto, which simply meant, the capital. Sometimes it was called the northern capital to differentiate it from the former capital, Nara. The city was laid out with great care and precision using a rectangular, square grid.

The emperor Kammu lived in Heian from the end of 794. Emperor Meiji moved to Tokyo in 1869. For more than 1,000 years (from 794 to 1868) Heian was the capital of Japan. It was also the heart of Buddhism in Japan.

Jimmu Tenno

Jimmu Tenno (or Kamu-yamato-ihare-biko) is accepted as being the first mortal ruler in Japanese history. Early chronicles record his expedition in 607 B.C. from Hyuga to Yamato where he established his centre of power. Japanese legend has him descended from the sun goddess Amaterasu, through her grandson Ninigi, who was sent to govern the earth. On earth, he married a descendant of the storm god Susanowo.

A Shinto shrine was erected by the Japanese government in 1890 at the site of what is believed to be his burial place at Unebi.

Sesshu

Sesshu was an artist of the Ashikaga period and one of the greatest masters of *sumi-e* painting. From the age of 10 he was educated in calligraphy, painting and religion at a Zen temple. He moved to Kyoto in about 1440 where he studied under a famous artist named

Shūbun. Twenty years later, he became chief priest of a Zen temple at Yamaguchi. From about 1466 he began to adopt the name Sesshu (Snow Boat). In 1468 he went to China to buy Chinese paintings for people and to study at Chinese monasteries and was held in high esteem by the Chinese.

After he returned to Japan in 1469 he painted his most outstanding works using Chinese models and Japanese ideas. His paintings included landscapes, Zen Buddhist pictures, and screens decorated with birds, flowers and plants.

Prince Taishi Shotoku

Taishi Shōtoku was an influential ruler and author who lived from 573 to 621. He was a member of the powerful Soga family and second son of emperor Yōmei. He promoted Buddhism and Confucianism and brought new political, religious and artistic institutions to Japan. He sent envoys to China which opened the way for the exchange of ideas. He also managed to transfer power back to the imperial house from the feudal lords.

He also brought Chinese artists and craftsmen to Japan, adopted the Chinese calendar and built many highways. Land irrigation projects were also undertaken to help the peasants. He also built many Buddhist temples including what has become the oldest wooden structure in the world, the Hōryu-ji Temple at Ikaruga near Nara in 607.

He compiled chronicles of government which was the first book of Japanese history. Court ranks were established and each rank was differentiated by the wearing of a different coloured cap.

In 604 he wrote a "Seventeen Article Constitution" which was based on the Chinese system and changed the old ways of Japanese government. Shōtoku also worked for the spread of Buddhism in Japan, and upon his death was regarded as a Buddhist saint.

Nara

Nara was the national capital of Japan from 710 to 784. The city is noted for its many ancient Japanese Buddhist buildings such as the five-storeyed pagoda of Kōfuku-ji (Kōfuku Temple) and the Daibutsu, or Great Buddha which is the largest bronze statue in the world, standing 22 metres (77 feet) high.

Here also is the Kasuga Taisha, (the Grand Shrine of Kasuga), one of Japan's oldest Shinto shrines, the path of which is lit by more than 3,000 stone lanterns.

Empress Suiko Tenno

Suiko Tennō was the first reigning empress of Japan within recorded history. She was the wife of emperor Bidatsu who reigned from 572 to 585, and daughter of emperor Kimmei. Bidatsu was succeeded by emperor Yōmei who died shortly after. Feuding followed between three families, the Soga, Mononobe and Nakatomi. The Soga clan won the struggle and the emperor Sushun gained the throne. He was murdered in 592 and Sushun's younger sister Suiko became empress in her own right.

Buddhism became established in Japan during Suiko's reign and many aspects of Chinese civilisation began to be introduced.

Index

Acknowledgements

The author and publishers are grateful to the following for permission to reproduce copyright photographs and prints:

Australasian Nature Transparencies: (M.F. Soper) pp.12, 31, 33, (Silvestris) p.13 left, (Otto Rogge) pp.13 right, 26, 34; International Society for Educational Information, Tokyo, Inc. pp.9, 27; Ronald Sheridan/ The Ancient Art and Architecture Collection: cover, pp.10, 14, 21, 22, 23, 24, 28, 36, 39; Werner Forman Archive pp.15, 16, 17, 18, 19, 25, 29, 32, 35, 37, 38, 40, 42.

Cover design and maps: Stephen Pascoe

First published in Australia by
THE MACMILLAN COMPANY OF AUSTRALIA PTY LTD
107 Moray Street, South Melbourne 3205
6 Clarke Street, Crows Nest 2065

Published simultaneously in Great Britain in 1989
by Macmillan Publishers Limited,
4 Little Essex Street, London, WC2R 3LF.

Associated companies and representatives throughout the world

British Library Cataloguing in Publication Data

Odijk, Pamela
  The Japanese.
  1. Japanese civilisation, to 1185
  I. Title II. Series
  952'.01

  ISBN 0-333-52086-6

Set in Optima by Setrite Typesetters, Hong Kong
Printed in Hong Kong

Oceania

Europe

Africa

c50 000 B.C. Aborigines inhabit continent

40 000 Evolution of man

Australian Aborigines	Maori	Melanesians	Greeks	Romans	Angles, Saxons & Jutes	Britons	Vikings	Egyptians	First Africans

8000 — Torres and Bass Straits under water / The Baltic — freshwater lake / Farm settlements

7500

7000 — Lake Nitchie settled / Neolithic Age, Settled agriculture

6500

6000

5500

5000 — South Australian settlements / Egypt-early farms / Increased trade across Sahara

4500

4000 — Hunting and gathering

3500 — Ord Valley settlement / Predynastic

3000 — Bronze Age / The first farmers

2500 — Crete — palaces / Old Kingdom, Giza pyramids

Mainland building

2000 — Megalithic monuments raised / Middle Kingdom / Sahara becomes desert

1500 — Bronze Age / New Kingdom

1000 — Dark Age / Farms and buildings established / New Kingdom declines / Kushites

Colonisation / Rome found / Persian conquest / Nok

500 — City-states established / Republic established / Ogham alphabet in use / Celtic Iron Age / Greek conquest / Greek influence

Classical Age / Rome expands through Italy and foreign lands / Roman Iron Age / Roman rule

Wars — lands extended

B.C. / A.D. 0 — Hellenistic Age / Roman invasion, Britain becomes two provinces

Legend: Kupe found New Zealand and told people how to reach there / Empire divided, lands lost. Culture enters new phase / Empire begins: Augustus — emperor / Hengist and Horsa arrived in Kent / Kushites' power ends

500 — End of Western Roman Empire / England: 12 kingdoms / Saxons settle / Vendel period / Army invade England / Arabs settle east coast

1000 — Maori arrive / Europeans dominate / Athelstan rules all England / Christianity adopted / Viking laws recorded / Christian European slave trade

Dutch explorers sight Aborigines / Cook's voyages / Norman Conquest

1500 — Great Britain annexed New Zealand / Europeans divide Africa

First White settlers / Christianity is introduced

2000